I0440399

United States Government Accountability Office

Report to Congressional Committees

August 2014

EXPORT-IMPORT BANK

Monitoring of Dual-Use Exports Should Be Improved

GAO-14-719

August 2014

EXPORT-IMPORT BANK

Monitoring of Dual-Use Exports Should Be Improved

Why GAO Did This Study

Since 1994, Ex-Im has had the authority to facilitate the financing of U.S. exports of defense articles and services, provided that it determines these items are nonlethal and primarily meant for civilian use. These "dual-use" exports include aircraft that are used by foreign militaries mainly for humanitarian purposes. After a 9-year hiatus, Ex-Im financed three dual-use exports in fiscal year 2012. These three transactions account for $1.03 billion, or just under 3 percent of Ex-Im's $35.8 billion financing for that year. Federal law requires GAO to report annually on the end uses of dual-use exports financed by Ex-Im during the second preceding fiscal year. This report (1) examines how Ex-Im has complied with its requirements for monitoring the end uses of the dual-use exports it financed in fiscal year 2012 and (2) identifies what dual-use exports, if any, Ex-Im financed in fiscal year 2013.

What GAO Recommends

To improve oversight for monitoring dual-use items, Ex-Im should strengthen its guidance for monitoring end use in cases where borrowers do not submit required documentation within specified time frames. Ex-Im agreed with GAO's recommendation and said it would revise its guidance.

View GAO-14-719. For more information, contact Kimberly Gianopoulos at (202) 512-8612 or GianopoulosK@gao.gov.

What GAO Found

The Export-Import Bank of the United States (Ex-Im) has policies for monitoring the end use of defense articles and services it finances, including documentation requirements that are reflected in its financing agreements with borrowers. However, these policies do not specify what actions Ex-Im officials should take if the bank does not receive the required dual-use-related documents. The requirements for each transaction vary, but may include (1) progress reports on construction and delivery, (2) technical operating reports, and (3) an annual certification and report on end use. As of July 31, 2014, Ex-Im had received most of the information it required in its credit agreements regarding the three dual-use transactions it financed in fiscal year 2012, but some of the information it received was late (see figure). For example, Ex-Im received

- some but not all of the progress reports required for the satellite transactions with Eutelsat and the Mexican government, and some information from the government of Mexico was more than a year late;
- the required technical operating report from Eutelsat, but only one of the two required reports from the Mexican government; and
- the annual certification and reports required from the governments of Mexico and Cameroon late.

Ex-Im officials told GAO they made efforts to obtain missing documentation for all three transactions, and, because of their prior vetting of the transactions and the details they had received, they did not think the missing documentation risked the exports being used in a lethal manner or for primarily military purposes. However, GAO found these efforts were often not timely and documented. Ex-Im therefore did not have complete and timely information about whether the items were actually being used in accordance with the terms of the agreements and Ex-Im policy.

Ex-Im did not finance any exports under its dual-use authority in fiscal year 2013, according to Ex-Im officials and Ex-Im authorizations data.

Status of Ex-Im's Fiscal Year 2012 Dual-Use Export Transactions

Item financed	Satellite for French company, Eutelsat	Three satellites for the government of Mexico	Construction equipment for the government of Cameroon
Status	Launched satellite handed over to Eutelsat in Sept. 2013 and Qatari government in Nov. 2013.	One satellite launched in Dec. 2012 and handed over to the Mexican government in Feb. 2013; the remaining two scheduled for launch by Mar. 2016.	Equipment shipped to Cameroon military and put to use on a rolling basis in 2013.
Progress reports	Received late or not at all.	Received late or not at all.	Not required
Operating reports	Received on time.	Received late or not at all.	Not required
Annual end use report	Not required	Received late.	Received late.

Sources: GAO analysis of Ex-Im documents; photos (left to right): Dynamic Graphics, © 2012 Orbital Sciences Corporation. Hoffman International, Inc. | GAO-14-719

_____ United States Government Accountability Office

Contents

GAO

U.S. GOVERNMENT ACCOUNTABILITY OFFICE

441 G St. N.W.
Washington, DC 20548

August 28, 2014

Congressional Committees

Since October 1994, the Export-Import Bank of the United States (Ex-Im) has had the authority to facilitate the financing of U.S. exports of defense articles and services, provided that Ex-Im determines that these items are nonlethal and primarily meant for civilian use.[1] These "dual-use" exports include items such as aircraft that are used by foreign militaries mainly for civilian or humanitarian purposes. As of July 2014, Ex-Im has financed a total of $1.67 billion in dual-use exports, with several transactions financed each year through fiscal year 2002. After a 9-year hiatus, it financed three more exports in fiscal year 2012: a geosynchronous satellite for a French company, Eutelsat S.A. (Eutelsat), manufactured by Space Systems/Loral, Inc.;[2] a fleet of three geosynchronous telecommunications satellites and related equipment and services from Boeing Satellite Systems and Orbital Sciences Corporation for the government of Mexico; and 150 pieces of new and used construction equipment from U.S. manufacturers exported by Hoffman International, Inc., for the government of Cameroon. These three transactions account for $1.03 billion in Ex-Im financing, or just under 3 percent of Ex-Im's financing for that year of $35.8 billion. The Mexico satellite transaction is the bank's single largest dual-use financing transaction to date, with a loan guarantee of $922 million.

Federal law requires GAO to report annually on the end uses of dual-use exports financed by Ex-Im during the second preceding fiscal year.[3] This report (1) examines how Ex-Im has complied with its requirements for monitoring the end uses of the dual-use exports it financed in fiscal year

---

[1] 12 U.S.C. § 635(b)(6). The Export-Import Bank Reauthorization Act of 2012 extended through September 30, 2014, the authority for Ex-Im to finance certain dual-use exports, which was first established in 1994 (Pub. L. No. 103-428, § 1(c) (Oct. 31, 1994), as amended by Pub. L. No. 109-438, § 4 (Dec. 20, 2006); Pub. L. No. 112-122, § 24 (May 30, 2012)). Ex-Im is authorized to use up to 10 percent of its total annual loan, guarantee, and insurance authority to support the sale of these dual-use exports.

[2] A geosynchronous satellite orbits the earth at the same rate as the earth's rotation.

[3] See the Related GAO Products section at the end of this report for a list of previous GAO reports on this topic.

2012, and (2) identifies what dual-use exports, if any, Ex-Im financed in fiscal year 2013.

To examine Ex-Im's compliance with its requirements for monitoring the end uses of the dual-use exports it financed in fiscal year 2012, and to identify what dual-use exports, if any, Ex-Im financed in fiscal year 2013, we reviewed Ex-Im documentation and interviewed Ex-Im officials in Washington, D.C. We conducted this performance audit from March to August 2014 in accordance with generally accepted government auditing standards. Those standards require that we plan and perform the audit to obtain sufficient, appropriate evidence to provide a reasonable basis for our findings and conclusions based on our audit objectives. We believe that the evidence obtained provides a reasonable basis for our findings and conclusions based on our audit objectives. For more information on our scope and methodology, see appendix I.

Background

Ex-Im is an independent agency operating under the Export-Import Bank Act of 1945, as amended. Its mission is to support the export of U.S. goods and services overseas, through the provision of loans, loan guarantees, and insurance, thereby supporting U.S. jobs. Ex-Im is generally prohibited by law from financing any credit sale of defense articles and services for any country. However, in an exception to this rule, Ex-Im was granted authority to facilitate the financing of U.S. exports of defense articles and services, provided that it determines that these items are nonlethal and primarily meant for civilian end use. Such items are known as dual-use exports.[4]

Ex-Im's Engineering and Environment Division, with assistance from the General Counsel, Congressional and External Affairs Division, and the Policy and Planning Division, is responsible for implementing the dual-use authority. According to Ex-Im's Military Policy, its definitions of "defense articles" and "defense services" are based on who the end user is, and then by the nature of the item and the use to which it will be put. In

---

[4]According to a senior Ex-Im official, "defense articles and services" is not defined in the law for purposes of Ex-Im's authority to finance dual-use exports, unlike other provisions of law in the Arms Export Control Act that define "defense articles and services" with specific reference to items listed on the United States Munitions List. Under Ex-Im's definition of "defense articles and services" for dual-use purposes, any article or service that is being sold to a military organization is automatically considered to be a defense article until proven otherwise.

addition, if the item is designed primarily for military use, it is presumed to be a defense article. For example, according to Ex-Im, furniture sold to a military organization for military use (e.g., for offices or homes occupied by military personnel) is deemed a defense article. However, according to Ex-Im, helicopters sold to a private firm or civilian police force are not defense articles. According to Ex-Im policy, an export is eligible for financing as a dual-use item if convincing evidence exists that the export is nonlethal in nature and will be used mainly for civilian activities. The determination of eligibility for dual-use financing may require applicants for Ex-Im financing to provide additional information beyond the contract and transaction data the bank normally requires for a loan or guarantee. Ex-Im may also seek to corroborate the information submitted by applicants by contacting other U.S. government agencies, such as the Department of State. For example, prior to approving the three fiscal year 2012 dual-use transactions, Ex-Im obtained written certification from each borrower that the items to be exported were nonlethal and would be primarily for civilian use. In addition, Ex-Im vetted the Eutelsat and Cameroon transactions with the Department of State, and vetted the Mexico transaction with the U.S. embassy military attaché in Mexico.

Ex-Im End-Use Monitoring Requirements in Credit Agreements Are Not Being Fully Met

Ex-Im has policies and procedures for monitoring end use, including various documentation requirements, which are reflected in its financing agreements with each of these borrowers. The documentation requirements for each transaction vary, but there are three types: (1) progress reports on construction and delivery of the exported item, (2) technical operating reports once the item is in use, and (3) an annual certification and report on end use. Ex-Im may also conduct end-use inspections, according to the terms of its credit agreements. As of July 31, 2014, Ex-Im had received most of the information required in its credit agreements regarding the status and end use of the exported items from the three borrowers approved for financing in fiscal year 2012 under the bank's dual-use authority, but some information was received more than a year late. Figure 1 shows the status of each of these transactions and the end-use monitoring of the exported items. Ex-Im officials told us they made efforts to obtain missing documentation for all three transactions. They also said that because of their prior vetting of the transactions with the Department of State or Defense and the details they had received about the transactions, they did not think the missing documentation risked the exports being used in a lethal manner or for primarily military purposes. However, we found these efforts were often not timely or documented. Ex-Im therefore did not have complete and timely information about whether the items were actually being used in accordance with the terms of the credit agreements and Ex-Im policy.

Figure 1: Status and End-Use Monitoring of the Three Fiscal Year 2012 Export Transactions, as of July 31, 2014

Item financed under Ex-Im dual-use authority	**Satellite** for French company, Eutelsat	**Three satellites** for the government of Mexico	**Construction equipment** for the government of Cameroon
Status	• August – November 2013: Launched into orbit, completed in-orbit testing, and handed over to Eutelsat and Qatari government.[a]	• December 2012 – February 2013: One satellite launched, tested, and handed over to Mexican government. • February 2015 – March 2016: Remaining two satellites scheduled for launch, and are therefore not yet in use.	• January – December 2013: Equipment shipped to Cameroon military and put to use on a rolling basis.
Progress reports on construction and delivery of financed export	◔ **Required**[b] – Monthly reports were due between June 2012 and November 2013. ◑ **Received late or not at all** – Two reports received in July 2013.[c]	◔ **Required**[b] – Four reports due to date; first was due by September 2012. ◑ **Received late or not at all** – One *draft* report received in May 2014; the other 2 not received.	⊖ Not required.[d]
Technical operating reports detailing end use	◔ **Required**[b] – First report due February 2014. ◕ **Received on time** – February 2014.[e]	◔ **Required**[b] – Two reports covering launched satellite due to date; first was due April 2013. ◑ **Received late or not at all** – One technical operating report, combined with revised progress report, received in June 2014; the other report not received.	⊖ Not required.[d]
Annual end use certification and report	⊖ Not required.[f]	◔ **Required**[b] – First report due April 2014. ◑ **Received late** – In May 2014	◔ **Required**[b] – First report due April 2014. ◑ **Received late** – In July 2014.
End use inspections (including of books and records)	• At Ex-Im's discretion – None to date.	• At Ex-Im's discretion[g] – None to date.	• At Ex-Im's discretion – None to date.

Sources: GAO analysis of Ex-Im documents; photos (left to right): Dynamic Graphics, © 2012 Orbital Sciences Corporation, Hoffman International, Inc. | GAO-14-719

[a]Ex-Im did not finance the parts of the satellite owned and operated by the government of Qatar's state-owned telecommunications operator, ictQatar.

[b]Required in the credit agreement.

[c]These reports were dated July 30, 2012, and January 11, 2013.

[d]Ex-Im requires progress and technical operating reports when supporting the construction of a specific project or asset. The Cameroon transaction was an equipment sale and did not involve the fabrication of any assets.

[e]The second report was due by the end of July 2014.

[f]There is no annual certification requirement in the Eutelsat agreement; Eutelsat is a private commercial entity with no military end use.

[g]According to the credit agreement, Ex-Im officials may inspect records regarding the end use of the satellites, provided the government of Mexico does not consider the inspection a breach of Mexico's national security.

Ex-Im Has Policies and Procedures for Monitoring End Use

Ex-Im has a detailed 1997 staff memorandum on dual-use policy for military applications, and Ex-Im officials confirmed that there have been no changes or updates to this policy. This memorandum tasks the Ex-Im engineers assigned to monitor dual-use transactions with "determining a reasonable and effective method to meet this monitoring requirement" that generally includes submission of periodic reports on end use, certified as accurate by the buyer, until the loan or guarantee is repaid, and could include periodic site visits by Ex-Im officials. In addition, the memorandum states that credit and guarantee agreements for dual-use transactions should include provisions for "progress reports" and "technical operating reports" to monitor the status and usage of dual-use items. Such information helps inform bank officials and provides them greater assurance about the exports' end use. The memorandum also includes provisions for action should Ex-Im find a violation of the dual-use policy.[5] However, the memorandum does not specify what actions Ex-Im officials should take if the bank does not receive the documents required in the agreements.

[5]According to the memorandum, "If the engineer determines that the buyer misrepresented the intended use, he/she should communicate this immediately to the Vice President of the Engineering and Environment Division and to the Office of the General Counsel so that appropriate action can be taken which may include accelerating repayment of the transaction, administrative actions or sanctions according to the nature of the loan and/or suspension of the buyer from access to future Ex-Im Bank financing."

Ex-Im's Policies and Procedures Are Reflected in the Financing Agreements for Each Dual-Use Export Transaction

According to Ex-Im officials, each of the credit agreements was negotiated on a case-by-case basis to incorporate the specific circumstances related to the borrower and the item(s) being exported. These credit agreements are legally binding on Ex-Im and the borrower, and each includes different provisions to ensure that end use could be monitored. The credit agreements for the two satellite transactions require the borrower (Eutelsat or the Mexican Ministry of Finance) to submit to Ex-Im (1) periodic progress reports covering the satellite(s)' construction, launch, and in-orbit testing; and (2) technical operating reports that include information concerning the operation and maintenance of the satellite(s) and related telemetry, tracking and command stations, and transponder capacity and use.[6]

The credit agreements with the governments of Mexico and Cameroon require an "Annual Certification and Report." Specifically, the borrower is to have the end user (the Mexican Secretariat of Communications and Transportation, and the Cameroon Directorate of Military Engineering) certify that the exported items have been and are being used primarily for civilian purposes.[7] This certification is to occur within 3 months after the end of each calendar year, starting by April after the year in which a first use is made. For the government of Mexico, this means that since one satellite was launched and became operational in 2013, the first report was due by April 2014. The report accompanying this certification is to include a list and description of tasks for which the satellite was used, including a summary of the civilian and military uses and the number of terminals allocated to and in use by any military organization or division of the government of Mexico.[8] For the government of Cameroon, the first report was also due by April 2014, since the equipment was shipped and put to use in 2013. This report is to include a list and description of tasks for which the equipment was used, the duration of each task, and a summary of their civilian and military uses, including the respective percentages of civilian and military use.

---

[6]A transponder is a device that transmits signals automatically when it receives certain predetermined signals. Each transponder handles a particular frequency range (also referred to as bandwidth). There are multiple transponders on a satellite, each capable of supporting one or more communication channels.

[7]The Cameroon Directorate of Military Engineering is analogous to the U.S. Army Corps of Engineers, according to Ex-Im officials.

[8]Access to the satellite is controlled through terminals on the ground.

All three agreements call for the borrower to permit Ex-Im officials to make "reasonable inspections" of books and records regarding the use of the exported items, though no inspections have occurred because Ex-Im officials determined that due to the timing and nature of the transactions, conducting a physical monitoring trip prior to significant use would not be an efficient nor a justified use of taxpayer money.[9] All three agreements also say that failure to comply with the provisions set forth in the agreement (if not remedied within a specified grace period) shall be considered grounds for default.[10] In addition, the agreements with the governments of Mexico and Cameroon state that any false or misleading information submitted to Ex-Im shall be grounds for default. The agreement with Eutelsat states that any information "proven to be incorrect" shall be grounds for default if not remedied within 60 days. Officials noted that while the bank does have the option to declare a default and accelerate payments, this is not usually the best option, especially with sovereign governments, for issues such as late reporting.

Ex-Im Has Received Some Required Information More than a Year Late or Not at All

Ex-Im Did Not Receive All Progress Reports from Eutelsat within Required Time Frames but Received the Technical Operating Report on Time

Ex-Im provided a direct loan to Eutelsat to finance 45.5 percent of the purchase and launch of a satellite. The remaining 54.5 percent was purchased independently by Qatar's state-owned telecommunications operator, ictQatar.[11] The credit agreement with Eutelsat required monthly progress reports on the construction, planned launch, and in-orbit testing of the satellite, beginning June 30, 2012. These reports help officials determine when the satellite will go into use. However, Ex-Im received

---

[9]In the Eutelsat agreement, this applies only to the financed portion of the satellite.

[10]The specified grace period is 30 days, according to the respective agreements with the governments of Mexico and Cameroon, and 45 days, according to the agreement with Eutelsat.

[11]Ex-Im's Board of Directors' approval memorandum for the Eutelsat transaction indicated that of the 46 total transponders on the satellite, 40 were designated for civilian use—23 by Eutelsat and 17 by ictQatar. Ex-Im only supported the 23 Eutelsat transponders. The remaining 6 transponders, purchased by ictQatar and not related to Ex-Im support, were designated for military communication purposes.

only two of more than a dozen required progress reports. These reports were dated July 30, 2012, and January 11, 2013, and were not received until July 2013. They were titled "Monthly Progress Reports" and included detailed information on completed and planned activities, such as anticipated launch and in-orbit testing time frames. Ex-Im officials told us they determined that despite the requirement in the loan agreement, monthly reports were not necessary and they did not believe the missing information posed a risk. An Ex-Im official stated that detailed reports, such as these, which summarize information over a several-month period, are more useful than a series of monthly reports. However, Ex-Im officials could not provide us documentation of this decision or of their efforts to obtain late (or missing) reports. The official said that when the credit agreement was being drafted, representatives from the satellite's manufacturer told the bank they prepare monthly reports for clients; according to him, this is why the monthly reporting requirement was incorporated into the credit agreement. Once the satellite was constructed and launched and its in-orbit testing was completed, in November 2013, progress reports were no longer required.

Once the satellite is in use, the credit agreement with Eutelsat requires the company to submit semiannual technical operating reports. The first technical operating report is to be submitted 3 months after the satellite's "in-orbit acceptance date" (the date on which testing of the satellite in orbit is completed). According to a January 2014 letter from Eutelsat, the in-orbit acceptance date was November 4, 2013; Eutelsat submitted its first technical operating report on time, in February 2014. Thereafter, these reports are due by the end of January and the end of July each year, until the loan has been repaid (just over 10 years). Eutelsat also submitted documentation certifying that (1) the majority of the satellite's 46 transponders are for civilian use (meaning that Ex-Im can finance them); (2) the remaining 6 transponders dedicated to military use for the government of Qatar are nonlethal and, now that the satellite is airborne, cannot be modified to change their use; and (3) the bandwidth, or capacity, of these 6 transponders is less than half of the satellite's total transponder capacity. Ex-Im officials said that this information, together with prior vetting of the transaction by the Department of State, gave them confidence that this satellite is nonlethal and will be used primarily for civilian purposes. However, there was no formal documentation of this determination. Ex-Im officials noted that they only needed to look at the 23 transponders financed by the bank and that their support did not extend to any of the military transponders.

Ex-Im Did Not Receive All of the Required Reports from the Government of Mexico, and Some Information Was More than a Year Late

Ex-Im received only a few of the reports from the government of Mexico required in the July 2012 credit agreement, and some of the information in a report it did receive was more than a year late. Ex-Im officials received these reports only after contacting Mexican government officials in April, May, and June 2014—after we began our review—to obtain missing documentation regarding the status and end use of the satellites.[12] An Ex-Im official said that the Mexican government acknowledged that it has been delinquent in submitting the required documentation and that the government is working with Ex-Im to make sure that it fulfills the agreement's documentation requirements.

The credit agreement calls for the borrower to submit both progress reports and technical operating reports. However, since the launched satellite's final in-orbit acceptance date of February 14, 2013, Ex-Im has received only one combined report, dated June 20, 2014.[13] According to the agreement, the borrower should have already provided to Ex-Im

- at least two progress reports covering all three satellites prior to the February 14, 2013, in-orbit acceptance date for the launched satellite (in the third quarter of 2012 and January 2013);
- two more progress reports (in mid-2013 and early 2014) covering the remaining two satellites, which have not yet been launched;[14] and
- two technical operating reports for the launched satellite, in April 2013 and April 2014, that were due 60 days after the satellite's in-orbit acceptance date, and annually thereafter until the loan guaranteed by the agreement is paid in full.

The combined June 2014 report lists dates for various stages of construction, testing, and launch/planned launch for each of the three satellites (one fixed service satellite and two mobile service satellites).[15] It states that the fixed service satellite was launched 18 months earlier, on December 19, 2012; completed in-orbit testing (in-orbit acceptance) on

---

[12]An Ex-Im official said there were other Ex-Im communications with the Mexican government, but could not readily locate any documentation of these communications.

[13]The combined report incorporates information contained in a May 21, 2014, draft progress report received by Ex-Im on or shortly before May 30, 2014.

[14]Another report was due by the end of July 2014.

[15]Fixed service satellites provide service to a geographically fixed end user, such as a TV station. According to an Ex-Im official, mobile service satellites are of greater concern because they provide service to mobile end users, such as military personnel in vehicles.

February 14, 2013; and was handed over to the Mexican government on February 24, 2013. The ground equipment for this satellite, which is necessary for satellite use, was handed over to the Mexican government on December 5, 2013. According to the report, the satellite is currently operating as expected at about 19 percent of capacity. The report also states that both mobile service satellites have been built and are in storage awaiting launch; one has an expected launch period of February 14 to March 15, 2015, and the other a contracted launch period of October 1, 2015, to March 15, 2016. Since these satellites have not yet been launched, they are not yet in use, and therefore do not yet need to be monitored for end use. Nevertheless, prior to receiving the June 2014 combined report, Ex-Im had no documented information regarding the status of the three satellites since the Ex-Im board approved the Mexico satellite transaction in May 2012, and none regarding the launch and operation of one of the satellites.

Finally, with regard to the third type of requirement, Ex-Im received the first required annual certification and report in May 2014, about a month after it was due. This document, dated April 28, 2014, consists of a two-paragraph letter and a two-page annex listing the terminals for use by the satellites. The letter states that the percentage of terminals for military and civilian use continues to remain the same (40 percent and 60 percent, respectively), as noted in a March 2012 Mexican government letter to Ex-Im, submitted prior to the Ex-Im board approval of the transaction.

An Ex-Im official said that despite the late or missing reports, he does not consider there to be a risk of violating the bank's military policy under its dual-use authority because he is confident that the satellites are nonlethal and will be used primarily for civilian purposes. He said this is because the Mexican Secretariat of Communications and Transportation—and not the Mexican military—is operating the satellites, and the military will be using less than half of the terminals. The official also noted that this transaction was vetted by the U.S. military attaché in Mexico prior to board approval.[16] However, Ex-Im did not document that missing or late reports posed no risk.

---

[16]The U.S. military attaché noted that the satellite system is unsecured and thus is inappropriate for use in tactical and strategic missions. He also specified that the satellites will be used for primarily civilian purposes, which include activities such as drug interdiction, search and rescue missions, and communications in rural areas.

Ex-Im Received Required End-Use Documentation from the Government of Cameroon Late

According to the credit agreement, the first annual certification and report on end use of the construction equipment exported to Cameroon was due by April 2014. Ex-Im received this required documentation several months late, in July 2014. Ex-Im officials received the certification and report after reaching out, with reminders regarding the credit agreement language, to the bank whose loan Ex-Im is guaranteeing; the U.S. embassy in Cameroon; and the Cameroon Ministry of Finance. An Ex-Im official said he had also spoken informally with the exporter. In addition, the report is missing information. The credit agreement requires the borrower to provide the respective percentages of civilian and military use of the equipment, but these percentages are lacking. The report simply notes that some of the equipment (e.g., trucks) "have been used very little for military purposes" to transport military items to the north of the country.[17] There are references to additional military uses of the equipment, but Ex-Im officials reviewed the documents and other information and determined that the end user had demonstrated that use has been primarily civilian in nature, despite the lack of a formal percentage. Nevertheless, Ex-Im officials said they will continue to follow up on the information in the report as part of their ongoing end-use monitoring.

An Ex-Im official said that the equipment arrived in Cameroon in several shipments during 2013 and was put to use on a rolling basis between March and December of that year. Ex-Im received evidence of delivery in the form of photos of the equipment on site and in use during operator training, as well as the transcript of a speech marking the acceptance of the final shipment. Officials noted that Ex-Im could conduct a site visit to verify the presence and use of the equipment for this project, but, given the photos, speech, and prior vetting of the transaction by the Department of State, there have been no indications of issues that suggest a special trip is needed. Nevertheless, an official stated that Ex-Im is discussing a potential visit to Cameroon within the next year to visit other (nonmilitary) projects involving road and bridge construction, and that if this trip takes place, Ex-Im officials may take the opportunity to visit the headquarters of the Cameroon Directorate of Military Engineering to inspect records of the maintenance and use of the equipment, as well as a list of sites where it is being used. If some of the sites are close by, officials may visit them.

---

[17]The northern part of Cameroon is subject to a State Department travel advisory because the Boko Haram terrorist group is active in the Far North of the country and there is a continuing threat of kidnappings and other armed attacks in the area.

Ex-Im Did Not Finance Any Dual-Use Export Transactions in 2013, Based on Application Data and Ex-Im Reviews

Ex-Im did not finance any exports under its dual-use authority in fiscal year 2013, according to Ex-Im officials and our review of relevant data on Ex-Im authorizations. According to Ex-Im officials, each application for financing requires the entry of numerous data elements for the application record. Several of these elements relate to whether there are any military implications in the application, and one field relates to whether or not the application would go forward under the bank's dual-use authority. The Engineering and Environment Division, which administers the bank's military policy and consequently its dual-use policy, is responsible for filling in this data field.

According to Ex-Im officials, Ex-Im's Engineering and Environment Division finds that roughly 70 percent of all requests for financing of military items under the dual-use authority have no credible civilian application; the division therefore deems these requests ineligible for financing. The remaining requests, those that the division formally identifies as eligible under the dual-use authority, are considered for approval by the board, which serves as an additional level of review. After preliminary board approval, the House Committees on Appropriations and Financial Services and the Senate Committees on Appropriations and Banking, Housing, and Urban Development are notified 15 days before the dual-use transaction is returned to the board for final approval.

Conclusion

This is the first time in almost a decade that Ex-Im has financed dual-use defense articles and therefore been required to monitor the end use of these exports. Ex-Im vetted these dual-use transactions before approving them and incorporated its policies and procedures for monitoring end use in its credit agreements. These requirements in the credit agreements include submitting periodic technical and annual reports documenting the status and end use of the items being financed in order to help officials determine whether these items are nonlethal and are being used primarily for civilian purposes. However, we found that some of these reports were missing or late. Moreover, we found Ex-Im's attempts to obtain missing documents were often not timely, and records of these efforts were sometimes lacking. Ex-Im officials did not think the missing or late documentation posed a threat that the exports would be used in a lethal manner or for primarily military purposes, based on prior vetting and other information. Nevertheless, this determination was not documented, and Ex-Im did not promptly and consistently ensure that the terms of its credit agreements were being followed with respect to end-use monitoring. Ex-Im's policies and procedures for monitoring end use do not specify what steps bank officials should take when borrowers do not comply with the end-use documentation requirements in their credit agreements and risk being found in default. Without specifying such steps and following them consistently, Ex-Im risks not having reasonable assurance that the items it is financing are actually being used in accordance with the terms of the agreements and Ex-Im policy.

Recommendation for Executive Action

To ensure adequate and consistent oversight for monitoring the end use of dual-use items, the Chairman of the Export-Import Bank of the United States should strengthen Ex-Im guidance for monitoring end use. Specifically, Ex-Im should establish steps staff should take in cases where borrowers do not submit required end-use documentation within the time frames specified in their financing agreements and ensure that these efforts are well documented.

Agency Comments and Our Evaluation

We provided Ex-Im a draft of this report for review and comment. In written comments on the draft, which are reprinted in appendix II, Ex-Im agreed with our recommendation and stated that it would revise its guidance by adding specific instructions about monitoring end-use activity, documenting related communications, and actions to be taken if reports are not received in a timely fashon. GAO also received technical comments from Ex-Im officials. Ex-Im officials updated information on the Cameroon transaction and clarified information about the terms of the loan agreements and their responsibilities. We made changes to our report in response to these comments where appropriate.

We are sending copies of this report to interested congressional committees. We will also send copies to the President and Chairman of Ex-Im, the Secretary of Defense, and the Secretary of State. In addition, this report is available at no charge on the GAO website at http://www.gao.gov.

If you or your staff have any questions about this report, please contact me at (202) 512-8612 or GianopoulosK@gao.gov.

Kimberly Gianopoulos
Acting Director, International Affairs and Trade

List of Committees

The Honorable Tim Johnson
Chairman
Committee on Banking, Housing, and Urban Affairs
United States Senate

The Honorable Mike Crapo
Ranking Member
Committee on Banking, Housing, and Urban Affairs
United States Senate

The Honorable Patrick J. Leahy
Chairman
Subcommittee on State, Foreign Operations, and Related Programs
Committee on Appropriations
United States Senate

The Honorable Lindsey Graham
Ranking Member
Subcommittee on State, Foreign Operations, and Related Programs
Committee on Appropriations
United States Senate

The Honorable Jeb Hensarling
Chairman
Committee on Financial Services
House of Representatives

The Honorable Maxine Waters
Ranking Member
Committee on Financial Services
House of Representatives

The Honorable Kay Granger
Chairman
Subcommittee on State, Foreign Operations, and Related Programs
Committee on Appropriations
House of Representatives

The Honorable Nita Lowey
Ranking Member
Subcommittee on State, Foreign Operations, and Related Programs
Committee on Appropriations
House of Representatives

Appendix I: Objectives, Scope, and Methodology

To examine Ex-Im's compliance with its requirements for monitoring the end uses of the dual-use exports it financed in fiscal year 2012, and to identify what dual-use exports, if any, Ex-Im financed in fiscal year 2013, we reviewed Ex-Im documentation regarding its dual-use policy, including a 1997 memorandum on implementing that policy; Ex-Im documentation associated with each of the three dual-use transactions Ex-Im financed in fiscal year 2012; and data on dual-use determinations. In addition, we interviewed Ex-Im officials in Washington, D.C., who review applications for the financing of dual-use exports and monitor end-user compliance with dual-use requirements, including the Vice-President of the Engineering and Environment Division. We did not independently verify the information provided to Ex-Im. Through interviews with cognizant agency officials about Ex-Im's procedures for identifying and categorizing dual-use transactions in its Application Processing System, we determined that Ex-Im data were sufficiently reliable for the purpose of identifying the dual-use exports financed under Ex-Im's dual-use authority in fiscal years 2012 and 2013.

We conducted this performance audit from March to August 2014 in accordance with generally accepted government auditing standards. Those standards require that we plan and perform the audit to obtain sufficient, appropriate evidence to provide a reasonable basis for our findings and conclusions based on our audit objectives. We believe that the evidence obtained provides a reasonable basis for our findings and conclusions based on our audit objectives.

Appendix II: Comments from the U.S. Export-Import Bank

EXPORT-IMPORT BANK
OF THE UNITED STATES

August 8, 2014

Kimberly Gianopoulos
Acting Director, International Affairs and Trade
U.S. Government Accountability Office
Washington, D.C. 20584

Dear Ms. Gianopoulos:

Thank you for providing the Export-Import Bank of the United States ("Ex-Im Bank" or "the Bank") with the Government Accountability Office (GAO) report, "Monitoring of Dual-Use Exports Should Be Improved" (August 2014). The Bank appreciates the GAO recommendation regarding the timeliness of reporting documentation. The Bank supports the GAO's work and audits which complements the Bank's efforts to continually improve its practices and procedures.

The GAO report made one recommendation as follows:

To ensure adequate and consistent oversight for monitoring the end use of dual-use items, the Chairman of the Export-Import Bank of the United States should strengthen Ex-Im guidance for monitoring end use. Specifically, Ex-Im should establish steps staff should take in cases where borrowers do not submit required end-use documentation within the timeframes specified in their financing agreements and ensure that these efforts are well documented.

Ex-Im Bank management agrees with the recommendation. The Bank will revise the existing Bank memorandum, "Implementation of Ex-Im Bank Dual-Use Policy for Military Applications" by adding specific instructions regarding the monitoring of end use activity pertaining to items covered by transactions approved under the Bank's dual-use authority. The language will include instructions on documenting contacts with any transaction party that is a source of required information relating to the end use of dual-use items and specific actions to be taken if reports are not received in a timely fashion. In addition, there will be instructions to ensure that any end use reports are adequately tracked.

811 VERMONT AVENUE, N.W. WASHINGTON, D.C. 20571

Ex-Im Bank appreciates GAO's professionalism and courtesy throughout this audit.

Sincerely,

Charles J. Hall
Executive Vice President and Chief Risk Officer
Export-Import Bank of the United States

Appendix III: GAO Contacts and Staff Acknowledgments

GAO Contact

Kimberly Gianopoulos, (202) 512-8612, or Gianopoulosk@gao.gov.

Staff Acknowledgments

In addition to the contact named above, Adam Cowles, Assistant Director, and Kay Halpern made key contributions to this report. In addition, Ashley Alley, Martin De Alteriis, Karen Deans, Etana Finkler, and Hai Tran provided technical assistance and other support.

Related GAO Products

Export-Import Bank: Financing of Dual-Use Exports. GAO-13-628R. Washington, D.C.: May 29, 2013.

Export Promotion: The Export-Import Bank's Financing of Dual-Use Exports. GAO-12-628R. Washington, D.C.: April 12, 2012.

Export Promotion: The Export-Import Bank's Financing of Dual-Use Exports. GAO-10-1052R. Washington, D.C.: September 15, 2010.

Export-Import Bank: Financing of Dual-Use Exports. GAO-13-628R. Washington, D.C.: May 29, 2013.

Export Promotion: The Export-Import Bank's Financing of Dual-Use Exports. GAO-12-628R. Washington, D.C.: April 12, 2012.

Export Promotion: The Export-Import Bank's Financing of Dual-Use Exports. GAO-10-1052R. Washington, D.C.: September 15, 2010.

Export Promotion: The Export-Import Bank's Financing of Dual-Use Exports. GAO-08-1182R. Washington, D.C.: September 30, 2008.

Ex-Im Bank: The U.S. Export-Import Bank's Financing of Dual-Use Exports. GAO-07-1234R. Washington, D.C.: September 27, 2007.

Export-Import Bank: The U.S. Export-Import Bank's Financing of Dual-Use Exports. GAO-01-1110R. Washington, D.C.: August 31, 2001.

Export-Import Bank: The U.S. Export-Import Bank's Financing of Dual-Use Exports. NSIAD-00-231R. Washington, D.C.: September 1, 2000.

International Affairs: U.S. Export-Import Bank's Financing of Dual-Use Exports. NSIAD-99-241R. Washington, D.C.: September 1, 1999.

International Affairs: U.S. Export-Import Bank's Financing of Dual-Use Exports. NSIAD-98-244R. Washington, D.C.: September 1, 1998.

U.S. Export-Import Bank: Process in Place to Ensure Compliance With Dual-Use Export Requirements. NSIAD-97-211. Washington, D.C.: July17, 1997.

GAO's Mission	The Government Accountability Office, the audit, evaluation, and investigative arm of Congress, exists to support Congress in meeting its constitutional responsibilities and to help improve the performance and accountability of the federal government for the American people. GAO examines the use of public funds; evaluates federal programs and policies; and provides analyses, recommendations, and other assistance to help Congress make informed oversight, policy, and funding decisions. GAO's commitment to good government is reflected in its core values of accountability, integrity, and reliability.
Obtaining Copies of GAO Reports and Testimony	The fastest and easiest way to obtain copies of GAO documents at no cost is through GAO's website (http://www.gao.gov). Each weekday afternoon, GAO posts on its website newly released reports, testimony, and correspondence. To have GAO e-mail you a list of newly posted products, go to http://www.gao.gov and select "E-mail Updates."
Order by Phone	The price of each GAO publication reflects GAO's actual cost of production and distribution and depends on the number of pages in the publication and whether the publication is printed in color or black and white. Pricing and ordering information is posted on GAO's website, http://www.gao.gov/ordering.htm. Place orders by calling (202) 512-6000, toll free (866) 801-7077, or TDD (202) 512-2537. Orders may be paid for using American Express, Discover Card, MasterCard, Visa, check, or money order. Call for additional information.
Connect with GAO	Connect with GAO on Facebook, Flickr, Twitter, and YouTube. Subscribe to our RSS Feeds or E-mail Updates. Listen to our Podcasts. Visit GAO on the web at www.gao.gov.
To Report Fraud, Waste, and Abuse in Federal Programs	Contact: Website: http://www.gao.gov/fraudnet/fraudnet.htm E-mail: fraudnet@gao.gov Automated answering system: (800) 424-5454 or (202) 512-7470
Congressional Relations	Katherine Siggerud, Managing Director, siggerudk@gao.gov, (202) 512-4400, U.S. Government Accountability Office, 441 G Street NW, Room 7125, Washington, DC 20548
Public Affairs	Chuck Young, Managing Director, youngc1@gao.gov, (202) 512-4800 U.S. Government Accountability Office, 441 G Street NW, Room 7149 Washington, DC 20548